Are you living the biggest scam called money?

Demonetization and after

Sachin Mittal

ZORBA BOOKS

ZORBA BOOKS

Published in India by Zorba Books, 2017

Website: www.zorbabooks.com

Email: info@zorbabooks.com

ISBN Print Book - 978-93-86407-31-3

ISBN eBook – 978-93-86407-32-0

Zorba Books Pvt. Ltd. (opc)

Gurgaon, INDIA

Printed at Repro Knowledgecast Limited, Thane

Table of Contents

PART I

Demonetization and After

In 1946, RBI declared 1,000 and 10,000 rupee notes illegal and then re-introduced them, to again declare them illegal in 1978 when they introduced 500 and 1,000 rupee notes. In 2016, again, 500 and 1,000 rupee notes have been declared illegal and new 500 and 2,000 rupee notes have been introduced. Plans to launch a new 1,000 rupee note as a replacement for the old one are also being considered, as of March 2017. There's something that makes us all wonder—can't the RBI, one of our apex financial institutions, make up its mind about what it really wants to do with our currency?

> *At the stroke of the midnight hour on 8th November 2016, the Government of India declared 500 and 1000 rupee notes— two of the most widely used denomination of our currency—illegal.*

People in India could no longer use their 500 and 1000 rupee notes for trading in goods and services. To replace these notes, new 500 and 2000 rupee notes were introduced. A large chunk of people's cash was declared illegal. There were reports that in some villages, a 10 kg sack of groundnuts started being traded in return for a litre of oil, chilli powder, salt, jaggery, half kg of potatoes and onions. Ferry drivers in Sabarkantha, Gujarat, started transporting people across the river in return for milk. People were being paid their salaries in quantities of groundnut, bajra, maize, wheat, etc. Once again, the old age exchange economy sprung alive in many towns and villages in India.

Running after money

This event makes me wonder, aren't we living a life of paradox?

*The money that we work for day and night has become important
for our smooth survival, and yet, the same paper notes on which
we depend for our lives are so volatile that they can be
rendered useless so easily.*

The political causes and their ramifications that brought about this cash-trap situation are outside our scope. What's important is the question which is so obvious, yet so covert:

*Does the paper money we use have any value at all? Do they correctly
represent the value of our sweat and brains?*

Are we investing our energies in the right manner? And the most crucial of all – are our central institutions, whose rules direct our lives, equipped well enough to protect us and our rights?

Well, what can be a better time to reflect back on our currency issues than now, just after when India witnessed the strongest foundation of people's lifeblood—money—being shaken.

Chapter 1

Demonetization and the Panchtantra Tale

...because every picture tells a story.

Demonetization takes us back to the story of the crocodile and the boy, which often finds mention in the Panchatantra tales. Let's try to understand demonetization through this story.

Once upon a time, there was a small pond in a village which was home to many small fish and a crocodile. Although living in the pond together with the crocodile was a little frightening for the fish, both fish and crocodile enjoyed their individual lives nonetheless.

One day when the village was at the peak of spring season, a boy aspiring to be the leader of the village started pumping water out of the pond. 'Why are you doing that?' asked the fishes.

'Well', he said, 'I want to make the lives of fish easier by driving the crocodile out of the pond.' So he continued sucking water out of the pond. 'This way a little amount of water will be left for the fish and the crocodile will go away due to lack of water', he told the fish.

Fish bought his argument and were ready to bear some difficulties which were likely to arise. Due to a reduced amount of water in the pond, fish were not able to breathe properly, but they bore this inconvenience with courage in the hope of a better future. Now they were waiting for the crocodile to go away and for the rainy season to arrive so the pond could be full again.

The crocodile on the other hand, was also waiting for the rainy season to arrive and for the pond to fill up with water again. Until then, he decided to enjoy living on the land and make do with less water.

Both the boy and fish failed to consider that crocodiles could adapt to living on both land and water. The whole exercise of pumping water out of the pond only created troubles for the small fish, while the crocodile easily adjusted with the needs of the time.

Demonetization is similar to this futile exercise of pumping water out of the pond in order to drive the crocodile away, i.e. weeding the black money marketers out of the market. It wasn't adequately considered that only a small amount of black money circulating in the economy is in the form of cash and the remaining amount must would have already been converted into other forms of assets like real estate, jewellery, etc. It was claimed that demonetization would better the future of the common masses. Instead, the whole exercise proved troublesome, difficult, and in some cases life-threatening for them.

During these times, more than 86% of the currency notes in circulation were swept away from the market and were frozen overnight in order to eliminate the very little amount of cash held in the form of black money and counterfeit notes by terrorist and antisocial elements. Common masses were left in awe and frenzy of this move. They couldn't comprehend whether what was happening was good or bad for them. On the one hand, our leaders were talking about putting an end to black money, corruption and counterfeit notes by banning 500 and 1000 rupee notes and on the other, we found majority of our lifelong earnings saved in the form of 500 and 1000 rupee notes rendered valueless overnight. To top it all, more than a dozen people died in the process of getting their old notes exchanged for new ones at the banks and some had to wait for long hours in front of banks and ATMs to get their well-deserved 'white' money exchanged in return for the newly launched currency notes.

I am not here to recount once again what common people had to go through during demonetization; we all saw that, rather I am here to tell you the gravity of what we had to go through during the first fifty days of demonetization. It is not the first time that a government took its people for granted. Time and again, common people all around the world have been forced to live an illusion of being protected under governmental institutions. This isn't about political leanings, I am no political mouthpiece trying to turn you against one party and in favour of the other. I have no political agenda whatsoever. It's about hitting the nail at the right spot. It is about knowing the fundamentals of our system and developing our understanding. It is about critical thinking. It is about asking questions. The capacity to think and reason is the single most important faculty that humans have, and in the midst of so many forces trying to turn us into robots, we have lost the zest to ask questions. I am here to reveal what we have forgotten and to remind us of our freedom. We work day and night for these pieces of paper, which were demonetized, but what if these papers are a deception. What if these are not money? Which leads us to the question, what is money?

Chapter 2

Money vs. Currency

Know the value, not just the price.

Demonetization has unveiled the reality of many illusions that we have been living with for generations. This event has ripened our understanding and equipped us to be able to grasp many of the intricate and hidden aspects of our daily lives especially regarding money, that we work for. One of the vital information which is often kept hidden from the people is the fundamental difference between Money and Currency.

After the announcement of demonetization, when you went to the milkman to buy milk for your daily consumption, did he accept the 500 or 1000 rupee notes that you offered to him? Unless he was your friend, or was willing to stand in the serpentine queues in front of the banks to get these old notes exchange for new, the milkman wouldn't have accepted them.

Now let's consider, would he have accepted a gold or silver coin in exchange for some milk? Of course, he would have. Though, you may say, why would you give him a silver or gold coin anyway. After all, it's so precious and you wouldn't trade it for milk. Well, that's an argument that we will consider in the later stages. My point here is that the shopkeeper, the milkman, or whomsoever you deal with, would have readily taken a gold or silver coin in exchange for the things you wanted to buy, but they would most definitely have refused to take 500 and 1,000 rupee notes, since they were declared illegal by the government.

Can government declare gold or silver illegal? No. They cannot declare them illegal in the same way as they cannot declare consuming bread illegal. It is because these are useful commodities and they will always remain useful, no matter the age, era or epoch we exist in. Gold and silver were legal and were as much tradable in the sixteenth century as they are today.

*The paper notes and coins we use are only a 'medium of exchange' that we use for buying and selling things which have an intrinsic value (commodities, such as bread, milk, etc.). These paper notes and coins are called **currency**.*

Money, unlike currency, has a value of its own. Precious metal and other commodities which were, or can be, used for exchange is called **money**.

Money can only be used as a medium of exchange, but it also has an intrinsic value.

The Rupees, Dollars, Euros, Pounds, etc. which we have in our pockets today is not money.

These paper notes that we use and work for are currencies. They are all designed to lose their value.

We will see later, how our governments and banks can go on to print these currencies and lower their value the moment a new lot of currencies enter the market (Inflation). This is called devaluation. It robs us of the value of our money instantly, just as a thief steals our wealth overnight. Coming back to the difference between money and currency, let's understand it in detail.

CURRENCY	MONEY
Properties and Functions of Currency	*Money possesses all the properties that are possessed by currency, but it has its own value as well.*
i) Currency is a **medium of exchange,** i.e. it can be exchanged for other valuable goods like milk, house, sofa, etc.	Money, can very well be called as currency, but it has an extra quality which makes it valuable over all mediums of exchange – it has a 'store of value'. That is, money can be used as a medium of exchange. It is a unit of account, it is portable and durable, but most of all – it has a 'value in itself'.
ii) Currency is **a unit of account**, i.e. it can be divided and can be used to measure the value or costs of different goods and services.	
iii) Currency is **portable**, i.e. it can be easily carried from one place to another.	*For example, a hundred rupee currency note is not worth hundred rupees in itself. Without government backing, it is merely a piece of paper. It takes less than five rupee to print one hundred-rupee note. Recall how 1,000 and 500 rupee notes were rendered useless overnight. They fetch goods worth that much amount because they have government backing. However, a gold coin is money. It has a value in itself. Its value cannot be snatched away by a government order.*
iv) Currency is **durable,** i.e. it is long lasting and not so easy to damage.	
Consider a hundred-rupee note. This note, i.e. currency, implies that it can buy goods and services worth hundred rupees in the market.	
Currency is printed and minted.	There are only so much of precious metals on earth. They can be mined and found, but cannot be printed and minted.

> *Precious metals, such as gold and silver, maintain their spending and purchasing power,*

i.e. they can buy same amount of goods over a long period of time because they cannot be printed or minted by the banks, while currency is designed to lose its value overtime because banks can print it on their whims and fancies. As a result, common people suffer inflation where prices continue to rise and our purchasing capacity keeps on decreasing. (We will study this phenomenon in detail later.) Our government can rob us of our purchasing rights when currency is demonetized because we trade in currency and the paper notes work only because our government and central bank give their backing to it.

Chapter 3

Scandalous Breach of Trust

When their house of cards crumbles, make sure yours is made of gold.

Whether demonetization has been able to curb black economy or whether it has impacted our GDP and economy, is not in our purview.

> *Here, we are considering the impact that this move has had on India's public institutions and how it has helped uncover the age-old scam going on behind the walls of these institutions.*

If there is any institution which bore the biggest blow from the government's arbitrary and botched-up operation of demonetization, it is India's central bank, i.e. Reserve Bank of India (RBI). Government effectively conveyed its intention of rooting out black money, corruption and counterfeit currency with this move, but in doing so it put in jeopardy the reputation of one of the oldest and authoritative institutions of India, i.e. RBI, the only institution conferred with the power to print Indian currency.

From where do currencies get their value?

In the previous section, we learnt about the properties and functions of currency. All the paper notes—Indian rupees, US dollars, euros, pounds, etc. —we use today are called currency.

> *These notes are not worth anything in themselves. If we have a hundred-rupee note, this paper currency gets its perceived value because it is signed by the governor of our central bank.*

If any government takes its backing away from these currencies, these notes will not be worth anything. It gets its value from government edicts. In olden days, these notes were backed by gold, which means that a hundred rupee note was backed by an equivalent hundred ounces of gold. So, if we went to banks and gave these notes to them, they would have given us the amount of gold it backed. But now, Indian rupee is backed by nothing but mere trust and good faith in our government. That is why these are also referred to as **fiat currencies**. Fiat means an order, decree, or sanction. Since these notes are backed by nothing but government approval/ order/sanction, they are called fiat currencies.

If you had witnessed and experienced the times of demonetization yourself, you may not need to ask why RBI was the biggest loser in this whole demonetization fiasco. But I will state it here anyway.

RBI issued as many as fifty-nine notifications changing the threshold of withdrawals and deposits which were permissible during the first fifty days of demonetization. Ad-hoc changes in withdrawal patterns, coupled with wedding season (marked by huge withdrawals) only fuelled the atmosphere of uncertainty in India. Logistical planning was totally missing on the part of central bank authorities. The decision to sweep away 86% of India's cash currency from the market diminished people's faith in the RBI and the currency. ATMs were not recalibrated with required plates equipped to dispense new and changed dimensions of 2,000 rupee notes. In addition, there was never enough cash in the ATMs and banks. They would close even before the half-day mark (1 p.m.). At some places, the queue waiting to get their cash exchanged or withdrawn from banks and ATMs stretched for a kilometre. For more than a week, people could get either only hundred rupee notes or absolutely nothing. Worse still, RBI was not at all prepared to deal with the loss of 86% of currency and had not accumulated enough new currency to release into the market after demonetization.

The lack of preparations on the part of RBI, and the immense secretive and whimsical manner in which the Indian government carried out the demonetization raised serious doubts on the autonomy of RBI.

Since 86% of the currency was to be taken away, it obviously required a lot of preparations on the part of the RBI. However, the manner in which bank officials and RBI authorities handled the rate at which the new currency was being printed, it soon became clear that neither the RBI, nor the RBI Governor were informed well in advance about such a crucial policy decision. Consequences were huge, a prominent being immense cash shortage, which continued even after fifty days of the demonetization period. Intense cash shortage led to hampering of daily economic activities that involved everyone, ranging from a daily wage labourer to small—and medium-businesses. To top it all, many bankers, and even some RBI employees were caught indulging in illegal currency exchange practices.

> *Managing stability in the economy is the main function of RBI and it failed to perform these functions during demonetization, and miserably so.*

People's trust in the RBI and its policies were shaken. The extent to which RBI's independence exists in reality was brought into question. Public frenzies over mishandling shown by the RBI can be gauged by the barrage of criticism not only by the general public but also by former RBI governors and current employees, which obviously brought irreparable damage to RBI's reputation.

Till date, the RBI governor Urjit Patel has no statistical breakdown of how much demonetized currency has returned to the system, how much of that is black money and how much have Indians benefitted from this stunt initiated to help curb corruption and flush out black money from the market. Not only that, the last update which was made available stated that RBI has no record of sums even larger than Rs. 2.5 lakhs (the limit beyond which deposits are taxable) which were deposited in the banks.

Why maintaining trust in the institutions is important?

Modern monetary system relies on people's trust. Today's fiat currencies have any value at all because people have trust in their governments and because governments have given their backing to these paper notes and coins. To let economies function, maintenance of trust in central bank – which has the authority to print money – is vital. It should be a major concern for any modern-day country that has its economy based on fiat currencies.

If the common man ceases to trust the currency, the central banks, the government officials, will lose power over the masses. We may cease to work hard to accumulate the paper notes. Especially when these can be printed so easily by the central banks and they continue to devalue our hard-earned money by adding more currency into the system via fractional reserve banking (explained in later chapters). Not only that, they can take away their backing from these currencies whenever they wish to do so (as happened in when demonetization was introduced in 2016).

This is why Larry Summers, leading American economist and former President Emeritus of Harvard University and Chief Economist of the World Bank commented on demonetization saying:

"This is the most sweeping change in currency policy that has occurred anywhere in the world in decades...legal tender to no legal tender essentially overnight. It is the imminent prospect of notes currently held becoming worthless that has created such alarm and disruption [amongst people] in India."

Similarly, Arvind Mayaram, IAS Officer and former Finance Secretary was rightly quoted in an interview with Asian Age:

"...the dollar has never been demonetized. The pound and sterling have never been demonetized. What they [government] are quoting [when they say even advanced economies demonetized] is withdrawal of silver dollar of 1887 or late 19th century but that is not demonetization which is what we are speaking of. None of the strong economic powers have done this because it shakes the confidence of people in the currency. Ultimately, the currency note is paper. Actually, the value of Rs. 1,000 note is Rs. 5 if you take the cost of its making. It becomes Rs. 1,000 because the RBI governor signs on it and says I promise to pay a sum of Rs. 1,000 if you produce it.

The credibility is there because everybody believes that when I will produce it I will get things or services worth Rs. 1,000. "

Even though economics seems more like a game of numbers, formulas and statistics, it is mainly driven by trust and beliefs of the general public. The purpose of the central bank is to remain strong, unbiased and rational when the government is on a downward spiral, to give an impression that it's doing something and not just filling its coffers.

Demonetization let the government portray that front very well to the public, but the uncertainties, irregularities and lack of preparation which was unravelled as this policy took effect, proved that the government didn't think about common masses at all and the RBI does not possess enough autonomy to question unreasonable moves made by the government.

What were the repercussions? Gold sales in India went through a spike after this announcement. With abrupt changes in government and RBI's notifications, public rapidly grew mistrustful of government's intentions and the currency started losing public trust. Eventually, people started to hoard Rs. 100, Rs. 50 and new currency notes as and when they got hold of them. To give you a small instance of the level of chaos and frenzy among people which prevailed during demonetization: The price of common salt which has always been under 20 rupees per kg, shot up to almost 250 rupees per kg due to rumours in various parts of India, claiming that there is a shortage of common salt in the market and its prices are soon to be increased to 500 rupees. Thousands of people bought common salt for 250 rupees per kg against the usual price of 15 rupees per kg.

This is a very small example of the kind of situation a loss of trust in governmental institutions can bring about.

As it becomes increasingly obvious to people that the institutions they have been working for and following the rules of have become completely corrupt and parasitic, it is bound to revive survival tendencies and thus chaos amidst people.

When governments and policies become more authoritative, it is essential not to be afraid. Identify the opportunity knocking on your door and try to understand it.

It is not the time to cower in fear, but the time to snap out of the delusions of currency that have been imposed upon us since ages.

Demonetization wasn't just poorly implemented, it also unveiled the true face and fragility of Indian institutions and currency that have been carefully hidden by the powerholders since long.

Chapter 4

The Desperate Case of 100 Trillion Zimbabwean Dollars

"You would have to pay for your coffee before you drank it because if you waited, the cost would rise within minutes."

~ Zimbabwean Businessman

Such is the flimsy condition of Zimbabwe's economy. Zimbabwe recently printed '100 trillion Zimbabwean dollars'. Yes, you read it right, 100 TRILLION DOLLARS, with fourteen zeros.

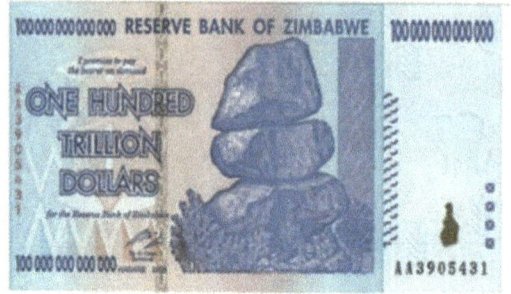

Its highly-inflated currency is the most eloquent symbol of the collapse of Zimbabwe. If you want to see how easily can a government destroy a currency, the real time example of Zimbabwe is worth reading about.

Under the Robert Mugabe regime, the state of Zimbabwe and its people has gone from bad to worse. In 1995, one US dollar was worth 10 Zimbabwean dollars and today one US dollar is worth 362 Zimbabwean dollars.

The Mugabe government went on to print more and more currency, thus rendering existing money supply totally worthless and continuously raising the prices of all the commodities in the market. It went into a printing spree so much so that, as of today, Zimbabwean dollar isn't even worth the paper it is printed on.

Zimbabwe broke the world record by lodging 132% inflation rate and months later the news of a launch of 100 trillion Zimbabwean dollars was made public. The new bank notes and the escalated notes that prevailed before it were not enough to buy anything, not even a loaf of bread. This kind of dictatorship stays empowered by printing money and crushing people's freedom.

100 trillion Zimbabwean dollars might be of even lesser worth than the paper it is printed on but it symbolizes something—the disruption—that it has in common with the Indian demonetization.

In a village in Zimbabwe, nobody was accepting Zimbabwean dollars, terming them worthless and volatile. People had started to trade in gold.

Even one hundred trillion dollar was not enough to buy a loaf of bread in Zimbabwe.

Reports also suggested that the authoritarian Mugabe Regime declared newspaper a luxury item and imposed 70% luxury import duty which made it unaffordable for an average impoverished Zimbabwean to buy it.

Back in 2009, the country's reserve bank, infamous for its printing spree and inability to counter hyperinflation, declared the US dollar as its official currency. Of course, the government couldn't keep up with that too.

To make their plight reach rest of the world, Zimbabweans and their press began printing their message on real Zimbabwean dollars. They have made posters out of real money. People started venting out their anger and despair on these dollar notes. Some don't even remember the last time they used the Zimbabwean dollar for buying or selling any goods or services.

Have we not been printing currency and constantly adding to money supply as well? Every country in this world has been. Otherwise, where do you think the bailouts and recapitalization packages from our central bank and government are funded from? These tendencies pose a real danger. The only difference being, we print additional money slowly and we (our central bank) claim to manage it well and keep the price rise under control. Irrespective of this management, it is for sure that the rupees, dollars and all fiat currencies in our pockets will continue to drop in value, i.e. after a period of time, this paper is going to buy less than it can buy today.

In the coming sections, we will see who has actually benefitted from demonetization and how it has put a dent in our purchasing power.

Chapter 5

Why Central Banks have the Monopoly over Printing Currency?

"The central bank is an institution of the most deadly hostility existing against the Principles and form of our Constitution..."

They say a diseased tree can never bear healthy fruit. Similarly, institutions that are designed to protect the rights and interest of the top few wealthy persons at the cost of the sweat and tears of the lower cadre cannot be expected to act in a rational and unbiased way. Would our government have declared our currency notes illegal with such ease if they were printed by many other agencies besides RBI?

Later in this book, we will see how the institution of central bank came into being and who it has been serving for all these years.

One main question that these economists, central bankers and our political leaders need to answer is, why is it that only central banks have a monopoly over printing currency?

In earlier sections, we went over how real money such as gold and silver has value irrespective of where it goes, whereas currency thrives on government's backing. How can we be assured that the government in power will not act upon its whims and fancies the way it happened in Zimbabwe? Can we trust a non-independent body (recently portrayed by RBI) to protect our right to property (with respect to the property of cash currency we hold in our pockets)? Especially when RBI nodded to government's orders and did not raise a single question? And most importantly, how can we give a government the right to declare our hard-earned money illegal overnight?

So, now say, is it worthwhile to give central banks the monopoly over printing currency since it doesn't seem to be doing the job it was created for (i.e. managing the currency supply)?

The main reason why common public fails to raise these questions is because throughout our lives, we have grown habitual to having a central bank and government around all the time.

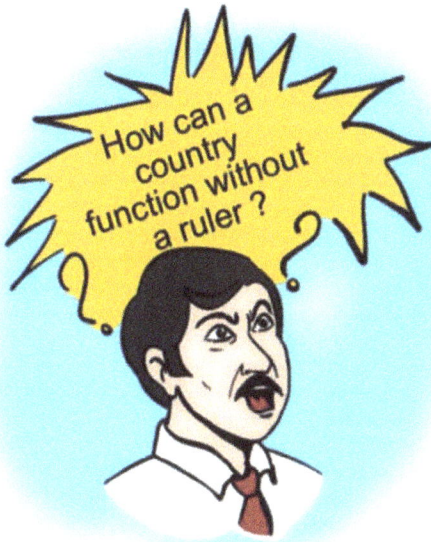

How can a country function without a ruler ?

It's similar to the situation when I was chatting with my second cousin who was then living in the parliamentary monarchy Nepal and I told her that India doesn't have a ruler at all. Even after twenty years, the look of surprise on her face is still fresh in my memory. She just couldn't buy the idea that any country can even function without a ruler.

Questioning becomes all the more difficult when there are almost no examples in the world where central banks have the monopoly of printing currencies (I cannot recall any!).

If central banks are to have the level of monopoly that they have, they should be able to justify the conferment of this monopoly via their performance. So let's put their performances to test.

This section will discuss and deconstruct how 'responsibly' RBI, India's central bank, acted at the time of demonetization.

During the global financial crisis in 2008, then RBI Governor D. Subbarao spent a good long five years chasing inflation and deflation, but was still always seen to be short of the target of controlling inflation and rising prices in the country.

Presently, the new governor Urjit Patel is taking the heat for something he had almost no involvement in. Important thing to be considered here is why was a policy directly impacting country's monetary system announced by the government and not by the RBI? Not only that, RBI didn't have a clue about it probably until just the night before. Additionally, there was no notification or discussion or invitation for academic papers (general modus operandi followed by RBI when pertaining to making big decisions) that was organised in preparation, during, or even after demonetization. This indicates how both the credibility and autonomy of our central institution RBI had already been compromised.

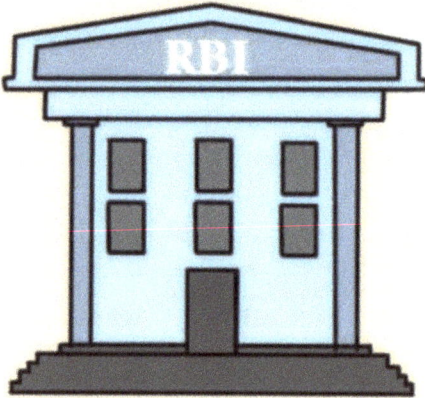

Another indication of RBI losing hold over the government is the non-befitting RTI reply in which RBI has suggested that the advice of RBI officials was not even properly sought by the government before taking this decision. If our government got away with this when the decision was directly related to India's monetary policy management, we can imagine how easily they can surpass RBI on other matters of public importance! It reflects a culture in our country where not even apex institutions – RBI or even Supreme Court – can save us from the coming adversities.

Finally, RBI has been suspiciously silent on the issue of demonetization. It has never been this silent on other matters pertaining to public trust. No open conference or explanation of why it was done and what has been achieved from it has been given until now. It shows a very uncharacteristic lack of concern on RBI's part with regards to the declining trust of the masses on India's currency and RBI's autonomy.

As I have stated earlier, ultimately, the real question is not whether demonetization was good or bad for the country. We should dig deeper into more fundamental questions about our banking system, the necessity of its existence and its working. Does the government or central bank deserve any monopoly over printing currency? Are they performing up to the mark?

Both RBI and government have been time and again attacked by Indian and international economic community on demonetization. The move of demonetization and many others before it – the role of US Federation in 2008 global financial meltdown, thousands and crores of bailout packages given to the failing banks, the depression in 1930, India's balance of payment crisis in 1991, etc. – have always proven the inadequacy of an individual organization or an individual to effectively respond to systemic problems. So, coming to our larger question: Would the government had been able to demonetize if there were many issuers of Indian currency and none had the monopoly over printing currency? The answer is an obvious 'no'. They would have to announce the plan only after convincing every currency seller and once a thorough discussion with them had taken place.

Traditionally, almost all central banks including 'independent' banks have proved bad in predicting money flow in the market and have never been able to keep themselves away from currency debasement (printing) and inflation.

So, where can we put our trust, market mechanisms cum competition, or RBI's single-handed management of Indian currency? Well, that's a big question to contemplate and I will leave it on the readers to decide until we reach the end of this book.

Chapter 6

Rise and fall of Private e-Gold Company

"Power does not corrupt. Fear corrupts...
perhaps the fear of a loss of power. "

~ John Steinbeck

What happens when the monopoly of money creation is taken away from the government? What happens when another authority is brought in between?

This is the story of the pioneer of the world's first successful e-commerce company, a digital currency operator backed by gold nonetheless, and coder of a successful online payment system using latest technology of SSL connections and APIs. We are talking about the iconic e-Gold, a private US company. It is essential to note the kind of rocky relationship they had with the US bankers and regulators (the government) ever since they had effectively taken away the government's right to issue currency.

Started in 1996, this industry leader was brought down by the regulators in the year 2008. e-Gold's daily transaction of precious metals was worth more than 2 billion dollars and it had more than five million users at the time it was shut down by the government. What were the events that conspired to shut it down? Let's find out.

e-Gold was founded by Douglas Jackson (pictured above), a doctor by day and coder in the night and Barry Downey, an attorney. e-Gold allowed its users to open their bank accounts on its website in the denominations of gold and silver (and some other precious metals). They could easily make transfers to other e-Gold account holders in the denominations of these precious metals only. e-Gold also allowed transactions as small as one-ten-thousandth of one gram of gold. At that time it was the only such successful micro-payment system.

Not just backing users' deposits in gold, the company also regularly published and showcased thousands of their micro-transactions and posted them live using API and other services providers. Along with this, a special page was devoted to recording statistical reports of e-Gold which showed holdings of each metal in e-Gold's account, the serial number of their gold bars, and total value of transactions on day-to-day basis. Such was the transparency ensured by e-Gold.

Through the ages, we have known how gold and silver have been a precious and worthwhile investment for people worldwide. Every time a fiat currency goes down, it is gold and silver that people depend on. The same phenomenon can be seen here. Soon, gold and silver not only intimated users but amplified their trust in their own savings, earnings and eventually in e-Gold company.

e-Gold was an outsider, a maverick in the banking system. Not only in the US, but it had created ripples and sent shockwaves to establishments all around the world. As it grew, this alternative banking system became a threat to the authority of central bankers and government.

Later on, e-Gold also became a target for some phishing scams, Ponzi schemes, and money laundering activities, the general banking system too suffers from these problems. But e-Gold's iconic status, immense success, alternative currency system and few political friends made it an attractive target for legal authorities of the US. Eventually it was brought to the courts of America and the powers had it wound up.

Like other countless entrepreneurs, e-Gold approached the world of internet with big dreams and eventually wound up in jail for twenty years and a house arrest because it had hit the core of government's power-stability dynamics. e-Gold wasn't even given any second chance or any bailouts and no government came for its rescue. Can you guess why?

Probably because Jackson envisioned bringing an end to the ills of modern monetary system. He endeavoured to blur the geographical boundaries and central bank monopoly characteristic of today's currency minting.

Though e-Gold failed to deliver then, it did lay the foundation for bringing currency innovation and gave an impetus to thinking in a manner that was never done before. e-Gold is often considered to have given a philosophical basis to Bitcoin, today's most secretive, most strengthened, and most prevalent digital currency.

Chapter 7

Ultimate Beneficiaries of India's Demonetization

"It reeks of a scam and has only ended up burdening the common folks with financial chaos witnessed across the country. "

~ AamAadmi Party (AAP)

"Access to your own hard-earned money had become burdensome... While common man was queuing up at the banks and ATMs, the crony-capitalists were unaffected by the chaos in the country's financial system. "

~ Valmiki Naik, Goa AAP Convenor

These were some of the reactions witnessed among all echelons of the society. Demonetization temporarily snatched away daily wages of more than 45 crores people in India who depend upon cash for their earnings. As per a newspaper report, more than fifteen crore of small fruit sellers and farmers suffered a great blow to their social and economic lives due to demonetization. Many of them even left for their hometowns since it became difficult to survive in their *karmbhoomi*, work cities such as Mumbai, Delhi, etc.

Isn't it amazing and hilarious how the Indian government declared that it will impose heavy tax penalties on deposits or amounts which were 'too large' (undeclared arbitrary figure) in quantity for the general public to deposit. On the other hand there surfaced many scandals showing how rich people managed to get thousands of crores of rupees exchanged in new notes (despite the exchange limit being 2,000 rupees per day and withdrawal limit being 15,000 per week) right in the first week of demonetization. Who helped them? And why were only the lives of common masses disrupted? What would you call this manner of execution of demonetization, if not authoritarian?

DID YOU KNOW? State Bank of India (SBI), one of the two systemically important banks of India, wrote off a debt worth more than 12,000 crores rupees of Vijay Mallya within the first week of demonetization. He was one of the top defaulters whose debt was written off by the SBI. It surely couldn't have come at a worse time, and it definitely symbolizes something. Now SBI's balance sheet is healthy again and it can go on to loan fresh currency to the borrowers.

Several arguments and even mathematical representations have suggested that demonetization will not be able to put any dent on more than 91% of black economy. Then the question arises, why was it done at all? Who benefitted from such shock-doctrine economics? What was the need to take up such a step, bound to bring more losses and economic distress than gains?

Let's figure out who were the main beneficiaries of demonetization and for whose welfare governments and central banks work for.

Do you recall Government of India's 'Indradhanush' program? Under this program, it was proposed that about 70,000 crores will be injected into the banking system by 2019 so as to improve the health of our banks who have been suffering from bad Non-Performing Assets (NPAs), unpaid loans and stressed assets. As a result, about 25,000 crores were injected into the banking system in July 2016 and now after demonetization, it has been proposed that only 10,000 crores more is required to recapitalize public sector banks and bring them back to their full health. Why is it that we now require lesser amount to recapitalize the banks is obvious to guess. In the month of November 2016 about 7,000 crores were to be given to SBI in a recapitalization package, but as a result of demonetization, right in the first week SBI received more than 5,300 crores as deposits and now apparently, they don't need those recapitalization packages anymore. Any doubts as to who are the ultimate beneficiaries?

> *Just before demonetization, RBI also declared that about 14. 5% of total loans given by Indian banks have become bad loans and thus declared them NPAs or stressed assets.*

Do you need any more indicators as to where our hard-earned money was going in times of demonetization? Okay, let's give you more. Let's look at some international reports published by International Monetary Fund. Recent Global Financial Stability report released by IMF shows the grim condition of Indian banks.

Basel Agreement is the list of regulatory framework released by IMF to direct banks to hold adequate capital and liquidity (cash reserves, gold, etc.) in their reserves in order to protect banking system from any unprecedented events or happenings. Basel norms direct banks as to what is the minimum threshold percentage of capital which is required to be kept by the banks. Let's see how India performs when stacked with other Asian countries in terms of Tier-1 capital reserves.

Tier-1 Capital

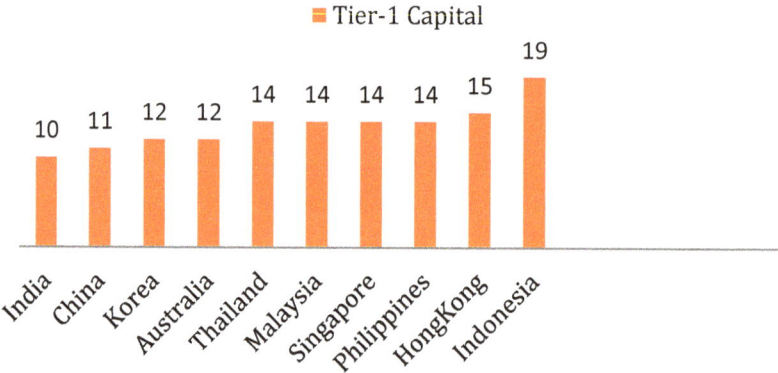

Bar chart titled "Tier-1 Capital" showing values by country: India 10, China 11, Korea 12, Australia 12, Thailand 14, Malaysia 14, Singapore 14, Philippines 14, HongKong 15, Indonesia 19.

Tier-1 capital, also known as risky capital, is the capital ratio required to be kept by the banks under Basel Agreement so that they can smoothly continue to function and are able to bear any financial calamity that may arise in future.

This also assures customers of the stability of their deposits. At present, India has the lowest risky capital reserves set aside amongst all other Asian economies. This shows that presently, Indian banks are not in a very healthy shape.

Similarly, India ranks second lowest among Asian economies in tier-3 capital reserves as well. Tier-3 capital is the reserves which are set aside to give protection to banking system against tertiary risks which come with foreign currency exchange, etc.

Point arises, if the intention of the Government of India was to recapitalize the banks and write off bad debts on their balance sheets, why did they not tell common masses about it?

Of course, the Government of India knew the grim situation in which our banks were. They knew we lack in tier-1 and tier-3 capital, they knew our NPAs are constantly increasing. They knew that the problem exists, but still they chose to carry on with demonetization instead of telling the public about the real condition our banks were in. Why? Well, when was the last time any government actually told the truth to the common people. Also, we have learnt in previous sections how important maintenance of public trust is for government and these central banks.

If they had told people about the dire condition these banks were in, there would have been consequences. Learning about the fragile condition of banks' balance sheets, people may have rushed to the banks and got their deposits withdrawn.

Then the government would have had to impose restrictions on withdrawals.

Well, you may say they did so even during demonetization. Actually, the temper of the public and the narrative sold by the government matters a lot. It directs people's trust in the institutions. In case of demonetization, RBI imposed limits on withdrawals because there was a high demand for currency in the market. However in case they would have told the people about the banks' grim situation, then withdrawal limits would have been imposed because there would have been a lack of money supply.

So now the mission to recapitalize has not only been successful but it has also been eased by people's money pouring into the banks.

It wouldn't be an exaggeration to say that rich people like Mallya went scot-free while suffering was the greatest for those whose lives completely depended on cash-based transactions.

After demonetization, people's declining trust in our country's financial services is not unprecedented. How can people have confidence in a government which sucked 86% of cash supply of the economy for the benefit of the top few? Trust barometer is bound to show the highest decline ever in people's trust towards its financial and governmental institutions, and most of all, the highest decline and loss of faith in the country's currency.

Chapter 8

Demonetization and Annihilation of People's Rights

No matter our job, our height, our class,
WE ALL DESERVE TO BE TREATED RIGHT.

Demonetization in India not only brought about exchange of old currency for the new one, but it also imposed the limits on daily permissible withdrawals. People waited in queues for hours to get their notes exchanged. Their economic activities were severely disrupted. Some left the cities for their home town since they could no longer survive due to lack of cash. About a dozen people also lost their life during this debacle.

Every press and newspaper brought to the fore the apathy of these people, but many failed to see the severe infringement of people's rights that was done by demonetization. Demonetization exercise is not something new in India. It has happened in 1946 and 1978, but both the times it was implemented after prior ordinances, a proper legislation process, and finally effected by parliamentary acts, whereas this time, even RBI was not properly consulted and no prior notification nor ordinances passed. This was a direct breach of people's constitutional rights and nothing short of emergency like conditions.

> *Similarly under article 360, unless financial emergency is declared, arbitrary limits on deposits or withdrawals of money cannot be randomly imposed on people. In the same manner, article 300 (A) gives us a legal right to own property. Government has no right to take away this property via an executive order. But still they did it and did it shamelessly.*

Neither any court, nor any newspaper raised any red flag there. Even the RBI did not offer any explanation for such a drastic move.

From their conduct during the demonetization period, what can we conclude about the effectiveness of these institutions? Do you think in times of financial emergencies these institutions can uphold our rights?

Chapter 9

Not the First Demonetization: 1946 and 1978

It's time someone takes accountability.

It is not like demonetization has never happened in India before, only that it has not been that drastic and hard-hitting as the demonetization of 2016. History does not give us any reasons to be optimistic about the exercise of demonetization, then why we did we go ahead with it? If history is to be our guide, Rs. 1,000 might soon be back into the system (as has been proposed by many already).

> *If pulling off demonetization is to be considered a perfect tool for curbing black money, then it can be termed as nothing but performing dialysis on the system. It is only a short-term cleansing for a long-term problem. If demonetization has to be done to keep black money at bay, then it has to be done again and again overtime. It will also be equivalent to betraying people's trust again and again. Should we say that our financial authorities will never learn from the past?*

It is not the first time that Indian government has taken its people for granted. The stunt of demonetization has been played twice in India in the past, in 1946 and 1978. However, one of the major differences between the past demonetization exercises and that of 2016 is that earlier demonetization was executed after following appropriate, constitutionally laid mechanisms, and central bankers were not informed only the night before implementing it. Let's reflect on India's encounter with demonetization.

1946 Demonetization Exercise

STEP TAKEN IN: January 1946

On 12th January 1946, the Government of India demonetized the Rs. 500, Rs. 1,000 and Rs. 10,000 denomination notes, and declared that they will cease to be a legal tender from then on. It was also done in an attempt to curb black marketing.

STATUS: The ban didn't really have much an impact on common masses because the notes of such high denomination were neither accessible nor hoarded by common people. However, these notes were again re-introduced into the market (due to inflation) and along with them, an additional Rs. 5,000 note was introduced in 1954. The ban could only impact black marketers for a very short time and obviously couldn't curb it altogether.

1978 Demonetization Exercise

STEP TAKEN IN: January 1978

In 1978, the Government of India once again decided to declare Rs. 1,000, Rs. 5,000, and Rs. 10,000 notes illegal via an ordinance and later it was enacted by the parliament in the form of High Denomination Bank Notes (Demonetization) Act. Back then too it was said that this step has been taken to curb black money.

STATUS: *1978 demonetization also didn't affect common masses to a large extent since these high denomination notes were not frequently used by the general public.*

Only a privileged few were impacted by this decision, and again, it didn't curb the presence of black money for a long period on time. An interesting point to note here is that then RBI Governor I. G. Patel openly expressed his discontent with this move. He strongly felt that this step was taken by the government only with an intention to immobilize funds of the opposition party. In his book, he has also said that he told the then finance minister that people didn't hold ill-gotten currency for too long. Therefore, hunting for black money only in the form of cash is myopia.

If in earlier cases demonetization was not a well thought process, at least previous governments didn't shake the foundation of the whole country by taking a decision that impacted about 86% of the currency supply. This time the repercussions have been close to dire. People died of shock, there were exceptionally big lines outside the banks and ATMs, black marketers made the most of it by offering to exchange old notes at the rate of 60% and 70%. There was an atmosphere of panic, and rumours abounded. Obviously, learning from history we can tell it can't curb black money for long and can neither keep counterfeit currency from reappearing.

Though as said earlier, there definitely is a big silver lining to this move. The condition of the government, helplessness of our central bank, fragility of our banking system, and volatility of our currency has come out in the open. India faces uncertain times, and repetition of this vicious cycle of currency banning and reintroducing has only set in motion a series of big questions people need to start asking. How can we work for these paper notes when the priority has always been to protect the elitist few and maintain the status quo for the government? Can we trust the bankers with our money? And the biggest of all, what is the role of this system in constantly reducing the value of the money in our pockets?

As disruptive as this move has been, we need to wake up from our decade old slumber and reconsider, if we can really trust the central bank and the government with our money!

To explore how these institutions got hold of our money and what are the real problems of our time, in the coming section we will study how our government and central banks are designed to rob us of the fruits of our hard work and value. We will see how the greed of few is being satisfied since centuries at the cost of the honest people. Last few sections will guide you on how to invest your sweat and hard work in the right manner. We will also discuss how every government and central bank in the world functions and how they are in cahoots with each other, only to loot us of our wealth.

The next section will open the doors to new knowledge about money. We always knew its reality. It was always right there in our face, but we never bothered to look into it. We will see how we can turn our problems into opportunities via this knowledge. Let's embark on the journey to understand money.

PART II

Are You Living the Biggest Scam Called Money?

Few subjects are as entangled and as confusing as money. Perhaps, such incoherent views on money stem from our propensity to live 'realistically', i.e. we only see and study the happenings of the immediate present. We are so intensely immersed in our lives that we forget to hold on for a while and understand our everyday affairs more fully. It is right in front of us and yet we have no idea about it. We are living the biggest scam of this century. It is constantly robbing us our intellect, ideas and creativity with each passing day.

It comes as no surprise to people a litre of milk we used to buy for one anna costs about Rs. 50 today. Why 10 grams of gold, which cost Rs. 88.62 at the time of independence, costs approximately Rs. 30,920 at present?

> *Why has the paper money we have been using since birth been constantly losing value?*

According to people, these changes 'just happen' because they have always happened. It seems so obvious. But is it? Is it *that* obvious? It is important that we stop running this rat race and ask ourselves, is this paper money we work so hard for worth anything after all?

This is the most important and yet a hidden truth of our age and century. People generally don't have the habit of questioning the validity of money, because we have never seen anybody doing so. Thus, we never question it ourselves. We have just been going with the flow. But what if this trend stops one day? What if people start asking questions?

The big banks and politicians rely on preventing thinking beings from asking the most basic yet pertinent questions about the fundamental unit of our economic system – MONEY. They do not want us to know about the theft that we have been subjected to for generations after generations.

We seek to unravel the technical jargon which has enveloped the concept of money, and break it down to make it understandable to every single human being. After all, It is our right to know everything about the thing we work so tirelessly for.

The biggest failure of our present system can be illustrated from the fact that one rupee note that carried a high value at the time of Independence, i.e. seventy years ago is worth only 0.2 paisa today. Talk about inflation!

It is colloquially said that inflation means rise in prices; but a more appropriate answer is:

Inflation means the value of money is coming down.

Chapter 10

Inflation and Money Supply:
What Really Makes You Rich?

Inflation is Taxation without Legislation.

Let's understand this phenomenon of Inflation in a little more depth, in order to understand its impact on our lives.

Assume that in 2006,

i.   You bought 10 grams of gold for Rs. 8,400, on one hand; and
ii. You kept the same amount of money idle as savings, on the other.

Let's see what happens to these two investments by 2016.

In 2016, the cost of gold has increased from Rs. 8,400 in 2006 to fluctuating somewhere between Rs. 24,910 and Rs. 32,336. While for obvious reasons (not so obvious, you will see) Rs. 8,400 in paper money remained same in numbers but decreased in value, i.e. if we could buy a sofa set with Rs. 8,400 in 2006, in 2016 it could only buy two wooden chairs probably. The sofa set has become too expensive for Rs. 8,400 in 2016. It is called inflation, i.e. rise in prices or decrease in the value of money.

Note: Money has no value in itself. Its value comes from its purchasing power, i.e. the things it can buy at any given point in time, such as number of TV sets, etc.

No matter how long you keep it idle for, it won't increase in numbers and will only decrease in value.

However, gold has a 'store of value', i.e. its shelf life is perpetual.

If we leave it idle, it will act as an investment and its value will definitely rise in the long term. Gold will continue to have some value irrespective of fall or rise of 'n' number of governments and irrespective of time and places we go to, while the paper money we use in one country will be useless in another, and unless it is invested somewhere, it has no 'store of value' in itself and not to mention, it can be declared illegal by the governments. These high prices of gold also indicate the deteriorating position of rupee in the market because now, our paper money is not worth as much as it was worth earlier.

Do you wonder why that happens?

When both gold and paper money are operating in the same market, then why is it that the paper money loses its value with time while gold doesn't? How is paper money different?

It happens because governments around the world continues to print money for various reasons—to fund wars, public works, credit funding, etc. Oh, now you must be wondering, if new money is being printed it should make us richer! Well, this is where paper money is different from other goods.

When other consumer goods, such as land, food, goods, etc., are added to the market, it brings prosperity and a higher standard of living for people, since more goods are now available given the same demand as earlier, thus causing the prices to come down.

While in the case of money, if more money is added to the existing supply of money, then more money is available for the same amount of goods present in the market. Thus, it increases the price of those goods and services. You will be better able to understand this phenomena from the example given below:

First Scenario

Supply Of Money   Goods In the Market

SUPPLY OF MONEY – 90 lakhs

For the sake of understanding, suppose in a particular market, the total worth of money in circulation is 90 lakhs and the goods in this market includes a house, a land, a sofa set and a TV. This means that 90 lakhs will be distributed amongst all the available goods, to determine their final prices.

Let's say, the house costs Rs. 60 lakhs, the land Rs. 28 lakhs, the sofa set Rs. 70,000 and the TV Rs. 1.3 lakhs in this market.

Second Scenario

SUPPLY OF MONEY (increased to) – 2 crore: Now let's say, the amount of money in circulation is increased (by printing more money) to 2 crores while, the number of goods, i.e. houses, land, sofa and TV, remains the same. What do you think will happen?

Supply Of Money   Goods In the Market

Since the supply of money has increased, this means more amount of money is available for the limited number of goods which are there in the market. So now, instead of 90 lakhs, the amount of 2 crore will be spread among these goods to cover their cost. Obviously, this will lead to an increase in prices of the goods available in the market. Or it can be said that the value of money will go down because 90 lakhs will not be able to purchase as much as it could earlier since more money is present in the market in this scenario.

When goods in a market increase, they confer social benefit.

But when money in circulation is increased, it increases the prices of the goods and decreases the purchasing power of money because in this case too much money starts to purchase (same or) limited number of goods.

What makes us rich is the abundance of goods in a market, not really the paper money we have in our pockets.

FACT: On an average basis, all the governments in this world have been constantly increasing the amount of money present in the system by printing more and more money – to fund wars, public works, etc.

This is why it is said that paper money is inherently inflationary. Since governments will continue to increase money supply and this in turn will inflate the prices, finally the value of our in-hand money is going to come down. But the question arises, WHY? Why are governments doing this to our money? Why they have been devaluing it? And the most important one, how did we come to value this paper currency so much when it's so inflationary? And why did we move to this paper currency when gold was available as a mode of transaction in earlier times?

Is it a trick to keep us satisfied and involved, only to disappoint us in times of uncertainties (like demonetization in India)? To answer these questions, we need to explore our relationship with money.

Hello! I am Money Genie. I will take you through the biggest truth of your lives.

We spend two most important aspects of our life – time and energy – in earning these pieces of paper we call money. We put 8-10 hours a day and our intellectual energies to work in order to earn these rectangular pieces of paper. Why have we come to value them so much? Will it help us survive in future no matter what?

Money is one of the first areas to be controlled by the governments all around the world. For centuries, they are being entrusted with the creation, distribution and regulation of money. Are they playing us? It's time we delve into the biggest questions of our time and pay attention to our lifeblood – MONEY.

We need to educate ourselves as to how this system is really working. We need to understand its operations, factor them and analyse them. Are we the beneficiaries, or the unintentional payers? Let's uncover some greatest hidden truths. They say, 'Past always lays traces for the future'. Let's go into the history of money and see how it came into being and how we reached where we are today. Let the game begin.

Chapter 11

Barter System

"I need your service and you need mine. Let's barter."

In the beginning, people didn't use paper money or even gold. Food and housing were the primary everyday requirements. Clearly, they couldn't eat gold or paper. There is evidence to show that they 'exchanged' goods and services. Exchange facilitated transfer of goods and services that one had for the goods or services of another person. They exchanged things they had, or they had made or found, in return for things they needed. Both parties benefitted in such an arrangement because each valued what they had received more than what they gave up. Say, I give up my fish in exchange for your wooden chair, that means I sold my fish to you because a wooden chair is more valuable to me at this point of time and similarly, you bought my fish because they were more valuable to you than your wooden chair. This system of exchange is known as '**Barter System**' or Exchange Economy.

As soon as humans started to cultivate the earth and become specialized in food production or other specific businesses, they started to settle down in one place for a long period of time and formed societies. Specializing in a particular production or business activity meant that we had to trade.

This is when we ran into the biggest problem posed by barter system, i.e. lack of 'coincidence of wants'.

Say, I want to exchange my fishes for your butter, but you don't want my fishes since you already have enough to eat. You want shoes instead. These sort of problems started to break societies.

If we wanted to specialize in a particular activity, we needed something beyond direct exchange of goods and services.

Coincidence of Wants and Indivisibility

Coincidence of wants is the foundation on which barter system or exchange economy can exist. Like in above examples, I can have your wooden chair, or butter, only when you want my fishes. Otherwise, we will be stuck. We will not be able to trade, will we? Or maybe, I can find someone who wants my fishes and is selling the shoes which you need. This way you can sell your butter to me, and I will give my fishes to the third person and he will give his shoes to you. Oh, imagine how much time trading will consume! This way, we won't be able to specialize anyway because all we will be doing is matching each other's demands.

This problem runs deeper when we are dealing with edible goods. Say, I want to sell my fish in return for your farm output, but your harvest only comes once a year. While I wait for you to reap your harvest, the fish which I caught today will rot in a few days.

Also, as early society started to own things and do business, there arose another problem of 'indivisibility'. Suppose, I need a cattle and I have fish to sell. No matter how much one values my fish, one would be very reluctant to sell their cattle in return for fish, since cattle was very valuable back in time. They might wish for a way to divide their cattle in four and sell me one of the pieces in return for fish, but unfortunately, then it wouldn't be of any use to them, since it would be dead by then (pun intended)! These problems soon started to grow bigger.

Even when goods were divisible, people would often run into a problem of coincidence of wants. And it became too gigantic a task for traders to find two people who would want each other's goods at the same time – a pure matter of coincidence, truly. So, humanity needed a universal third good, which would not only be divisible but also be wanted by everybody in exchange for trade. Then entered, MONEY.

Chapter 12

Emergence of Money

The function of Money in society is to bring Ease.

Anything can serve as a medium of exchange as long as we all agree, it has a value and it passes all three measures mentioned above. If everyone is sure that a third universal entity will be more readily sold and its demand is high, then we wouldn't have to search for people to exchange their goods for ours. They can simply sell this third good which is high in demand for their goods. The role of this third universal good came to be played out by money and soon it became widely used. This is how money became a **medium of exchange**.

In the process of trial and error, we have used several weird things as money. Tobacco was used at one point of time in colonial Virginia, Cattle in ancient Greece, and Copper in Egypt. We even used tea, grains, beads, etc. One of the widely used forms of early money was 'Cowrie Shells'.

They were durable and even impossible to counterfeit since they could only be procured by using modern harvesting technique.

These pre-modern forms of money were called 'Commodity Money'

since real commodities were used as a medium of exchange and most importantly all these commodities had value in themselves.

Two commodities which emerged as the king of them all were – Gold and Silver. Gold soon displaced all other forms of commodity money from the market. People felt secure and could feel the worth of gold, when it was in their hands. So, now if I hired Raghav and Sneha for building my house, I could easily pay them their worth of labour in gold or silver coins. And they could use these coins in the market to buy anything they want.

This way, with the emergence of money, we busted the problems of 'coincidence of wants' and 'indivisibility' that plagued our society due to the Barter System. But when an economy grows, it shows the limitations of the contemporary systems. Let's see how we came to use these paper notes instead of gold coins.

Chapter 13

Gold to Gold Currency

Gold is everyman's way to save.

As our economy grew, traders ran into further trouble. Nonetheless, commerce became very easy with gold, but gold often proved cumbersome to carry around in cases of massive transactions. Gold is a heavy commodity and it became a real pain in the neck to carry it from one place to another, especially across borders. Not only was carrying gold difficult, but since it was valued by everybody, it was also not safe to carry around hundreds of kilograms of gold. There were a lot of dangers involved – like the gold getting stolen, etc.

This is when goldsmiths offered people to keep their gold safe in their vaults or money warehouses for a tiny bit commission, and they could give some pieces of paper in return which had the amount of gold and the name of the depositor written on them. Besides, the depositor could come and redeem their gold in return of these receipts at any time they wanted. People accepted and this was how the very first 'IOU' (I Owe You) came into picture.

IOU is a promissory note in which the person/authority (at this point in time it was the goldsmith) who had depositor's gold promises the depositor to pay their gold back to them when they ask for it.

With the advent of IOUs, only the form of money supply was changed, but technically the exchange was still taking place in gold since IOUs still represented gold. People started to use IOUs and keep their gold with goldsmiths, since IOUs were considered as good as gold. Soon, everybody in the market had these paper receipts. Goldsmiths made a pivotal switch in these receipts at this time. They changed these receipts from 'redeemable only by the person who originally deposited their gold' to 'redeemable by anybody who held these receipts'. This is how the concept of bank and IOU was first introduced.

Convenience of keeping and carrying these paper receipts instead of gold soon lead to their usage even in general transactions. Instead of using pile of gold coins, people started to use these receipts as currency for transactions. And since each of these receipts were backed by gold coins, everybody had trust in them. Why go to the troubles of turning these receipts with banks, when you could just trade these receipts with other merchants for buying their goods and if they wanted, they could simply to go the banks to get their value in gold.

Say, Rahul and Sneha both have stored their gold in same money warehouse/bank. If Sneha buys a flower cart from Amit for 80 ounces of gold, so in this transaction, instead of going to the bank and redeeming her receipts, Sneha can simply handover her receipt of 80 ounces of gold to Amit. And if Amit wants, he can just go and redeem gold for this receipt from the warehouse/bank.

This is how **gold currency** was born. Every paper IOU was backed by gold. When these paper receipts began to be accepted almost by everybody in the market, depositors started to ask for receipts in different denominations – from smallest to highest, so that they could use these IOUs for buying different things in the market. It made trade far more convenient for people, and laid the foundation of paper currency.

So each IOU that bankers printed represented 100% gold. To keep the temptations of bankers in check, depositors were allowed to redeem these IOUs (liabilities) in gold on-demand. It was thought that this

Did you know ?

India's Central Bank RBI, was also a private entity until 1949, i.e. it was formed by a private body on 1 April 1935

1 April 1935

BANK

Private Entity

1949

RBI

India's Central Bank

provision would limit banker's greed to misuse the system by printing IOU's recklessly on their wishes and whims. As economy and political power of the society grew, government and bankers joined hands (almost everywhere in the world) to keep people's gold 'safe', and thus emerged the concept of 'central bank'. Before this, almost all the central banks or bankers were private entities. Some of those have still maintained their private status till date. Only the central banks were now responsible for keeping people's gold in reserves. This helped bankers and governments around the world in centralizing their functions and also in multiplying people's trust in this system.

CLASSICAL GOLD STANDARD
(1815-1914)

This was the period when every nation's currency (IOUs) were backed up by an equal amount of gold. That is why it is called the epoch of 'Classical Gold Standard'. This meant that each dollar, pound, rupee, etc. were only names for a certain ounce of gold that it backed. So, let's say, you have US $ 10. If you would go to the bank and slap this $ 10 on their table and ask for your gold, banks would give you 10 Ounce of Gold. This is what gave people confidence in these IOUs.

Chapter 14

Rush of Paper Currency

Self-destructive paper standard becomes rampant.

As soon as the IOUs started to circulate around and pass from hand to hand, the usage of gold in day-to-day transactions started to decrease. Bankers (former goldsmiths) soon noticed this phenomenon. They realized that the IOUs they created were being passed often without coming back to the banks to be encashed in gold. This meant that people's trust in these IOUs was immense and they considered these paper receipts as good as gold. Since so much gold always remained there in the warehouses, bankers were tempted to use that money for their benefit. They felt they could play around with money now.

Bankers thought that unless suddenly everybody wanted to redeem their paper receipts for gold at the same time, they can use the gold money in their vaults to turn in the money from other people. How? Through lending. They thought that while IOUs are circulating in the market, they could use the coins they represent to prompt others to give their money to them by proposing to lend to them. If they lend the money they had, then the borrower will not only be liable to give them the money bankers lent them, but borrowers will also give some extra interest (commission) on the money they borrowed. This way they could earn free money.

To earn free money, bankers started to print more paper receipts without any gold backing, i.e. they issued more paper receipts (IOUs) with the claims that they were redeemable in gold, but in actual there was never enough gold for these paper receipts that were floating in the market. So, in case of a sudden bank run, bankers were now in no position to give every depositor back the gold.

Banks printed more IOUs without any gold to back them in their vaults. Essentially, what the banks did was to issue pseudo receipts to the borrowers. So now, unless everybody wanted their gold back at the same time, they could simply go about doing this exercise of printing pseudo receipts and earn hefty income in return of printing more money. (What a job!) Printing pseudo receipts (equivalent to counterfeiting), instantly added to the money supply thus leading to rise in prices and inflation.

This was how the concept of **Fractional Reserve Banking** was born in its most nascent form. For example, if earlier the entire gold economy (every IOU backed by gold) was worth 30 million ounces, and bankers printed new IOUs worth 15 million ounces without backing them with gold, then the money supply would rise from 30 million ounces to 45 million ounces, while the effective goods and services in that market remain the same. Too much money chasing too few goods will eventually lead to inflation. This entire system is bound to collapse, until this hocus pocus is discovered by the public and they all ask for their gold at the same time in return for those paper slips (IOU).

Note: Whenever Banks issue new notes (IOUs), they add to the money supply. While, when businesses borrow or lend money, they do not. Why? It is because banks 'print' new notes and add them into the market, but businesses float the existing currency while enhancing its value by creating new goods and services.

Chapter 15

Gold Exchange Standard

The history of Gold is an account of abuse and mismanagement.

What were categorized as pseudo receipts until now were given an official form with the advent of World War I. By 1914, banks stopped all redemption rights in the name of war. It entailed that we could no longer go to the banks and ask for our gold in return of IOUs. Not only this, bankers lit up their printing presses to print more IOUs on the orders of the governments, back then. In a nutshell, gold of the common masses was held hostage, so 'great wars' could be funded and soldiers be paid. Since the bankers were already running out of gold in comparison to the paper receipts they were printing, governments and bankers decided to introduce Gold Exchange Standard.

> Under **Gold Exchange Standard system**, the paper currencies were decided to be partially backed by gold. Like, $20 worth of gold would back $50 worth paper currency, i.e. only 40% reserve ratio. So, when classical gold standard had 100% gold reserve ratio, gold exchange standard significantly reduced the reserve of gold which would back the amount of paper currencies present in the market.

People often ask, if the classical gold standard worked so well, why did it fail? In actual, it was not gold that failed, rather the mistake of trusting bankers with their promises of keeping people's gold safe. It was the mistake of entrusting governments with the task of making better monetary judgements that failed. Printing pseudo receipts and warring governments led to inflation of so severe levels, that it was impossible for bankers now to keep their promises. Thus, they went off the classical gold standard and declared their bankruptcy soon after entering the war.

USA didn't enter World War I during the entire war. Thus, it was the only country which didn't increase their supply of dollars. Rather, in this period, since almost the whole world was at war, it was only USA which was supplying all the essential goods (bread, butter, clothing, etc.) to other countries in return for their gold.

> Printing more currency is also known as devaluing, i.e. you are devaluing the worth of your currency. When gold and silver are devalued, this process is known as debasement.

According to the legend, during the Peloponnesian War within the Greek city-states, there emerged widespread inflation. The Greek rulers started mixing copper with gold coins. This obviously led to the reduced value of gold. So, even though the government held more coins now, copper severely reduced the value of gold. For general masses, this led to immense inflation. Metal was used as money by several empires and almost all (from smallest to biggest) of them debased their coinage at one point of time or another. Ironically, the image of the king was always stamped on these coins, which was a sign of trust in the system—that 1 gram of gold really is 1 gram of gold. In ancient India, these coins were called 'Pann'. In present day India, we use coins of Rs. 10, Rs. 5, Rs. 2 and Rs. 1 and all are metal money. Its manufacturing costs only 0.30 paisa to our government and still it fetches us a Cadbury Eclairs worth rupee one. This is an example of fiat system of money prevalent today (explained later).

Chapter 16

Bretton Woods: 1945

Even the slightest hinge to gold makes one feel safe.

Similar to World War I, even in World War II, USA didn't enter the war until the Pearl Harbour incident. It was at that point that USA placed its troops on the ground. Before that, it was only selling essential goods to other European nations like earlier, while others nations directed their economies to the war effort and paid USA in the form of gold for the imports they were making. By the time World War II ended, almost about two-thirds of total world's gold was with USA. Europe on the other hand, had none at all. So now the whole of banking and monetary system was on the verge of complete collapse, since no currency (except US Dollars) was backing any gold. Since USA had majority of world's gold and it had also loaned several thousands of dollars to Europe without gold backing, USA participated in Bretton Woods Conference, held in New Hampshire in 1944.

> *Main representatives from all around the world met here to discuss an alternative world monetary system which came to be known as Bretton Woods System.*

In this conference, it was decided that every currency in this world will be backed by the US dollar and in turn the US dollar will be backed by gold worth $35 per ounce. Surprisingly, this gave a great sense of confidence to all the currencies of the world, since now they were all backed by gold to some or the other extent. No matter how faint, lingering ties to gold still remained. The governments which came later surpassed these rules once again to print unregulated amount of paper currencies and led to the emergence of Dollar Standard or Fiat Currency. As usual, it wasn't possible for governments to limit their spending. USA did some good deficit spending itself for Korea and some other countries, i.e. it spent more than what it had in its gold reserves. This soon expanded the paper currency supply in the market.

Chapter 17

Rise of Fiat Currency: 1971

Welcome to the World of Irredeemable Paper Money.

USA was increasingly inflating its money supply and lending credit to other governments, while the shock of no gold in vaults after the Second World War taught many countries like Switzerland, France and Italy, to pursue 'hard money' policy. As a result, their economies started performing quite well and the production was once again bouncing back to normal. This led to the biggest deficit crisis in Balance of Payments for USA. How?

As 1950s and 60s wore on, the President of France, Charles de Gaulle, started to become suspicious about the credibility of piling up dollar. As their economic prowess grew, France decided to bring back their gold reserves. This act seriously impacted USA's economic affluence abroad. Other countries also started to jump on board and asked USA to give back their gold. By 1971, USA had lost about 50% of its gold reserves (going from 20 billion to 9 billion dollar) and the world at large still had 12 times more dollars than they had gold. It became clear that USA couldn't pay everybody their gold back and it may have to declare bankruptcy. Once again, the entire world monetary system was on the verge of collapse (like 1944) and there were chances that the gold standard might come back into use but that didn't happen.

The result of America's bonanza gave another death blow to the gold-linked monetary system in 1971.

*On 15th August 1971, new monetary system was launched which removed gold backing in any form. The few lingering links to the gold were broken now. It is also popularly known as **The Dollar Standard.***

Sensing bankruptcy and collapse, President Nixon in Unites States disallowed any country or company or individual to ask for their gold after 15th August 1971. This was the first time when every currency in the world became a fiat standard currency.

Under this monetary system, all currencies were now linked to dollar and gold backing of whatever amount was removed. Now none of the countries' currencies could be defined in terms of gold or redeemed in that form. The world's currency supply was now solely based on dollars.

Government paper (IOUs) now became fiat standard money. Money system was now at the mercy of governments and bankers. People were asked to bow down and consider these paper moneys as standard money.

This was how first fiat paper currency was born. People were asked to get over their absurd and tribal gold fetish. Bank deposits were no longer redeemable in gold. So now, governments could officially inflate (increase money supply) or deflate (decrease money supply) the economy on their whims and fancies. This move obviously insured all the central banks of the worlds and put these bankers at the helm of our economies; gold was shamelessly eliminated. This was how the banking systems were absolved from all of their mistakes.

It's not very surprising that this step didn't lead to any civil wars or widespread dissatisfaction of that sort. People by now, were already out of their 'habit' of trading in gold. Some even thought that these papers were still as good as gold and some simply forgot that paper currency had gold backing in any form. This marked the end of Bretton Woods System. Do you find this new system completely and totally bizarre? Wait till you get to the next section and see how our present system is actually working today!

Chapter 18

Fractional Reserve Banking and System at Present

Of all cheatings, none has been more delusional than paper money.

Henry Ford Senior once said, "If people understood the banking system, there would be a revolution before morning. " Even today, some people think that their currencies are as good as gold, or they are backed by some gold at least. But that's so not true. It hasn't been true ever since 1971. The Classical Gold Standard lies forgotten now and the fiat currency we use today has no gold backing whatsoever. Now, banks are allowed to create money from a system called Fractional Reserve Banking and this is what makes the present monetary system the biggest scam. Let's see how it works.

Money Creation with Fractional Reserve Banking

Do you know what happens when we deposit our money in the banks? Well technically, we don't really deposit our money, but allow bankers to lend our money to a borrower while keeping a small fraction of our deposits in their vaults for emergency needs and in return banks give us a teensy-weensy interest on our deposits. So after keeping required reserves in their vaults, bankers loan out their excess reserve to businessmen or anybody who is in need of money. These loans are offered in the form of credit cards, home loans, education loans, etc. On every loan they make, they charge a hefty amount of interest (far greater than they give to the depositors) from borrowers. These borrowers go onto spend this money, and then the person borrowers traded with, using the loaned money would go and deposit the money in the banks. Then again, banks will lend a major part of that money, while keeping the required reserve amount in their vaults. And this process continues.

Let's understand the working of fractional reserve banking system by an example.

Let's see what happens when you decide to deposit Rs. 1,000 into the banking system. For simplicity sake, let's assume there is a required reserve ratio of 10%.

Reserved INR 100/-   Loaned INR 900/-

BANK

Deposit INR 1000/-

Total Money Supply
INR 1900/- *Why?
*Depositor's Money = INR 1000/-
Borrower Has = INR 900/-

Reserved INR 90/-   Loaned INR 810/-

BANK

Deposit INR 900/-

Total Money Supply
INR 2710/-
Money Supply from Step 1 = INR 1900/-
New Borrower Has = INR 810/-

Reserved INR 81/-   Loaned INR 729/-

BANK

Deposit INR 810/-

Total Money Supply
INR 3439/-
Money Supply from Step 2 = INR 2710/-
New Borrower Has = INR 729/-

Process Countinue

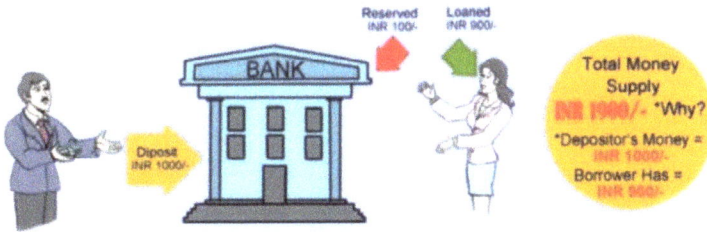

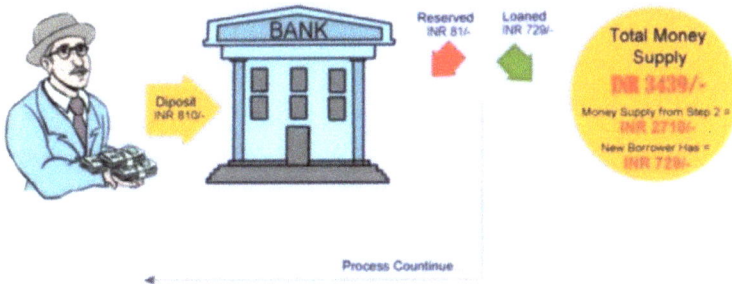

In the very first step, the deposit of Rs. 1,000 suddenly created new currency worth Rs. 900, subsequently adding to the total money supply in the market. Thus, total money supply becomes Rs. 1,900, while banks hold only Rs. 100 in reality in their vaults. Now, the currency that was borrowed by the borrower (Rs. 900) will definitely end up getting back to the bank, either directly by the borrower himself, or by some third person, the borrower will end up paying the borrowed amount. Whatever be the case, it doesn't really matter. For simplicity, we have assumed that it's the borrower who deposits back the borrowed amount. In this case, once again, the bank will loan all but 10% of the deposit (Rs. 900). Thus creating new money (Rs. 810) and adding to the money supply, while it has only 10% reserves to give back to the depositor in reality. (Does this remind us of the time goldsmiths printed pseudo receipts, or when banks ran out of money in the 2008 financial crisis?) And this process goes on and on.

Who said that only Central Banks could create money! Oops, I did sometime before. The new system of fractional reserve banking has completely changed how banking works. Now, indirectly every bank has the right to create money and add to the money supply, thus leading to inflation and price rise.

For every money that is being deposited, there is a whole lot of new currency that is being created. This is why they say, the present system is inherently inflationary, i.e. the prices are always going to rise. They may go down a little for short term, but on an average, in total, they are only going to rise. And the thorniest problem of fractional reserve banking lies in the fact that the money supply grows at a faster pace than the economy.

In India, this reserve ratio is determined by RBI and is known as **CRR (Cash Reserve Ratio)** and **SLR (Statutory Liquidity Ratio)**.

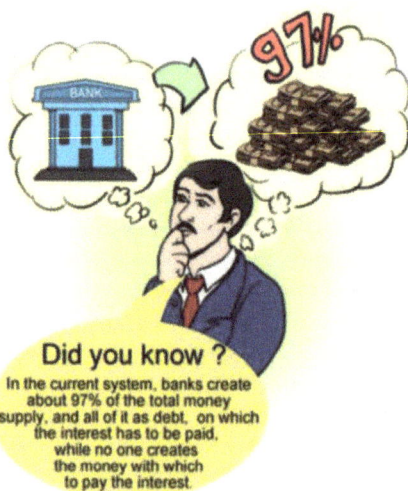

Did you know ?

In the current system, banks create about 97% of the total money supply, and all of it as debt, on which the interest has to be paid, while no one creates the money with which to pay the interest.

CRR is the percentage of deposits which should be kept aside by the banks as 'cash only' reserves. SLR is the amount of highly liquid assets like gold, government securities (explained later) which should be kept aside from a percentage of their deposits. SLR may include cash as well, but a higher percentage of assets other than cash should always be kept as SLR. It is because gold and government securities are considered highly safe assets.

Presently (as of February 2017), CRR is 4% and SLR is 20.50%. So this means, all banks have to keep at least 4% of their deposits aside in the form of cash and 20.50% in form of liquid assets like gold and government securities.

Today's paper currency money is but an illusion. The fact that we work for it for our whole lives makes it all the more bizarre. We work to earn money to pay our debts. Debts, for which the real money never really existed in the first place. However illusionary, this system will continue as long as this mirage continues. The only problem being, it is people like you and I who suffer the most. The harbingers of this system have safeguarded themselves from a long time ago.

This whole system became more insecure when governments joined hands with the bankers. These banks not only funded us by giving us credit, but major inflation is also injected into the system when whole governments and their welfare or war plans are funded by these bankers.

And guess who pays back the interest and principal amounts on these debts taken by the governments? Right! It's we who pay these debts, via taxes and other means.

Governments give this illusion that they are regulating, printing and managing the currency supply. But in reality, it's their central banks and bankers who have been doing that. You will notice that in almost all countries including USA and India, either these central banks are private or have a good amount of autonomy. Since our politicians tend to be not so economically sound, I cannot say whether that is a good thing or bad. But from what I can make of it, the whole situation seems totally hopeless.

People ask me what is the exact problem with it! They realize there is some problem, but they want somebody to state it in so many words. Imagine with gold as money, or 100% or even as some percentage of gold backing the paper currency, we could go to the banks, slap our papers and ask for our gold back. It would keep inflation in check because there was only a finite amount of gold available in the market. But now, nothing backs the paper currency we use. No matter what name you give to this fiat currency – Dollar, Indian Rupee, Franc, or anything – the underlying fact is that this paper currency provides for an open channel for unlimited inflation to occur in the market. Not to mention, it is a legitimate and legally 'manufactured' inflation.

The present system is working because we all believe it is working, but what if one day the trust of people breaks down in the system (recall the condition of banks in London during the financial crisis in 2008), or if governments get dismissed or a civil war breaks out. What will bankers give us in return for these paper notes? Nothing at all. They will simply declare themselves bankrupt. Would we be able to use our paper currency if we had to flee to some other country? No. Yes, we could get it exchanged at Forex. But there lies a big problem. Unless our economy is functioning well the exchange rate of our paper currency will go down significantly. For example, when Britain chose to exit European Union (Brexit), one British Pound Sterling decreased from Rs. 99 to about Rs. 75.

Such is the instant and significant impact on the 'value of paper currency', in case of any change that happens in the economy. So, this means, if earlier, one British pound could buy things equivalent to Rs. 99, after Brexit the same British pound could only buy things equivalent to Rs. 75.

Note: A Britisher earned one Britain Pound Sterling by selling same amount of his labour in both the times. Then, why did his purchasing power decrease at the time of Brexit?

So, finally I ask, what's the worth of this paper currency? It will render us hopeless in case of any unprecedented or sudden bad event. In general as well, its value will continue to go down due to the pace at which fractional reserve banking is adding to the money supply. Gold, on the other hand, retained its value, no matter in which land it went and no matter how bad the times were. Due to government meddling, gold did see some booms and busts, but it was always effectively managed in the long run. Common masses didn't have to suffer at the behest of some wealthy elites. If France printed more currency than there was gold, they had to suffer the consequences in international market and were ultimately forced to decrease their prices.

We have seen how governments and central bank took over the monopolized control of our money. And how new money has sprung into existence via fractional reserve banking. But how is it that this system seems so flawless to people? Why do people never question its authority? It's evidently so because we are largely ignorant about its working. We don't know how and from where our banks loan us the money that they do and how financial institutions including central bank have been regulating them.

> *To be able to see the reality of this system more clearly, it is important to understand and see the workings of these institutions for ourselves. How is it that the demand for money is made and what role do we play in this entire system? Let's see how our government, central bank and banks work.*

PART III

How Indian Monetary System Works?

Most of the truth regarding what goes behind the walls of our legacy institutions remains hidden from us because people don't really get to understand the working of this whole system. It's not unusual that you have a hard time figuring out the monetary system of the world. Undoubtedly, it is a little intimidating at first.

Right from my childhood I wanted to know how money is created, since I always wanted to know why our government can't make these poor people rich by giving them newly printed paper notes. Well, as I grew up, that myth and the possibility of it coming true got busted (refer to the section on inflation and case study of Zimbabwe's currency). Back then, I never fully understood how printing of money works, how different components of the system interrelate with each other, and how central bank really manages a country's monetary system.

As I started to explore the working of financial institutions and started to ask the right questions, one thing led me to another. And there was the truth, right in my face. Today, I can very confidently say that these big financial terminologies and circulation loops are only to confuse us. The whole system is very simple to figure out, if you see it from the right angle and don't let yourself get mystified by it. Let me decode our entire system for you. It is nothing but a big sham, complicated only to confuse common people and to keep them ignorant of what is conspiring behind those walls.

Let's see how all of this plays out. Almost every monetary system in the world works like this.

Chapter 19

What do Politicians do after they Win and Form the Government?

Oh! The harvest party is plenteous. The money will be managed.

Before winning an election and forming the government, politicians make big promises in order to lure their voters and mobilize them prior to elections. These promises are even documented in the election manifesto of each political party, which is published during their campaign. They make promises like, "Vote for me, I will ensure that your village gets constant supply of electricity, new roads are constructed, CCTV cameras are installed, and people below poverty line get subsidized ration, etc. "

When the time comes for them to fulfil the promises they had made to the public before elections, for this is the only way they will again be voted to back to power, they go to the treasury or finance ministry (in our case) and ask for money with which to build the roads, install CCTV cameras, etc. as they had promised it to their voters.

At this time, the finance ministry doesn't have any money, but they have one thing—the trust of more than a billion people (evident since they have been voted to power). So, what the finance ministry does is, they go to the country's central bank (RBI) which has the authority to issue currency and ask them for money to fund the government's projects for the general welfare of the public.

Recall how when we go to the banks and ask them to loan us money, the banks ask us for a guarantee or collateral and then give us a loan against that collateral. It is a form of security which ensures that the person who has taken the loan will pay it back in full with interest. In case they fail to pay it back, the collateral can be seized to recover the loaned money.

But when a country's government (via finance ministry) asks for money from its central bank, they don't have to put anything as collateral. Their biggest collateral is 'people's trust'. So at this point finance ministry issues a promissory note (IOU) which basically says, 'I Owe You' this much amount of currency and this much amount of interest. The Central Bank (RBI) takes this IOU and writes a check against zero balance and gives the government whatever amount they want, so the government in power can fulfil their promises; that is how the currency suddenly springs into existence. Henceforth, government uses its newly found currency to meet its expenditure commitments.

Note: The promissory notes or bonds or IOUs given by the government are considered risk-free instruments because they carry sovereign guarantee and are generally in the form of government securities (g-secs, Treasury Bills, Commercial Bills, etc.). These promissory notes or bonds or IOUs are given by the government to the RBI in return of which the RBI issues new currency notes to the government. Some government securities are long term instruments like government bonds which take more than a year or so to mature and some are short term, such as treasury bills.

> *This is why RBI is also called 'the Banker to the Government' because it is the only source from which the government of India takes internal loans. A government can also take international loans from World Bank, IMF and other foreign countries that are willing to lend.*

Can you guess who ultimately repays these loan made in the form of IOUs by our governments? Yes, it's us. Government earns its income via taxes which we pay. So essentially we repay these loans our government takes internally (from RBI) and externally (International Institutions or Foreign countries) through the taxes we pay. The loan amount that our government, essentially each one of the citizens, owes to varied institutions can be determined by knowing our country's **national debt**. In 2015, India's national debt was about 66% of its GDP.

> *This is not all. It is obvious that the amount of money our government spends always exceeds the amount of income it receives from taxes. If that happens, it is known as **fiscal deficit.***

It differs from national debt in the sense that national debt is the accumulation of all the debts upon us up until now (ever since we have started to take debts), while fiscal deficit represents yearly borrowings of government. With increasing national debt and increasing fiscal deficit, our future generations will have to pay more and more taxes. What essentially our government is doing is to steal the prosperity from our future, so it can spend it all today.

Chapter 20

What does the RBI do with Promissory Notes/IOU/Bonds (G-Sec, Treasury Bills, etc.) That It Receives from the Government of India?

It upholds confidence and brings prosperity to the government.

The bonds which are given by the government are then sold in an auction by the central bank. RBI, on behalf of the government of India, participates in the Money Market. It is nothing but a fancy term for the market in which selling and buying takes place between banks and various financial institutions.

various financial institutions

So, the IOUs or bonds given by government in the form of government securities like Treasury Bills, Commercial Bills, g-secs are put in the market for auction. Various commercial banks including Public Sector Banks like SBI, etc. and Private Banks like HSBC, ICICI, etc. along with other financial institutions participate in this auction process and buy these bonds-cum-IOUs from RBI.

Chapter 21

Why do Commercial Banks buy these Government Bonds and What do they do with it?

Keep Going. It's a Loop.

The IOUs or government bonds that commercial banks receive are used by commercial banks in three forms.

I.   One of the forms has been discussed before in Fractional Reserve Banking section, i.e. all the banks are required to maintain a certain percentage of their deposits in form of liquid assets called SLR and these mainly include gold and government securities. Buying these securities is not only competitive for commercial banks but also a necessity.

II. Second, the funniest and most often used manner in which commercial banks use the government securities is by taking short term loans on them from RBI. Commercial banks can keep these government securities as collateral with RBI and can take loans against them. So, essentially what is happening is that the RBI is giving out loans to both government and other commercial banks on the same IOUs. Basically all that is happening here is swapping of same government created IOUs between the government, RBI and commercial banks and that's how new currencies are being created.

III. These IOUs are also used by commercial banks to let common public invest in them since they are considered so-called 'safe assets' in financial markets.

Government

Other Commercial Bank

Yes, it's crazy. If you or I did it and made promissory notes or IOUs to get loans, we will be categorized as fools or frauds. However, the government and central bank can do it, because they have the monopoly over currency creation.

When the government spends all the newly minted currency on public works like hospitals, building roads etc., it also pays contractors, sub-contractors and labourers with the same currency. They then go to the commercial banks and deposit their money with them.

Note: As we have learnt before, when depositors deposit in commercial banks, they are not actually depositing their money but giving the rights to banks to lend their money to aspirant borrowers. This is called Fractional Reserve Banking System.

People deposit their currency with banks: they then lend it to others (after keeping in reserve a certain percentage of those deposits in the form of CRR and SLR). So now, when a person wants to buy a house on home loan, they will go to these banks, ask for loans and these commercial banks will give out their deposits in loans (after keeping the threshold requirement of CRR and SLR). The borrower's mortgage will also say, 'I owe you this much amount in principal and this much amount in interest'.

It is important to note here that the interest amount which will be charged to the borrower will be the highest amount of interest charged from anybody in this entire chain of swapping of IOUs.

Here is another ludicrous fact. Banks, which are essentially loaning the deposits made by depositors, are not loaning out the real currency which exists in the accounts. Rather, a new fiat rupee is created out of thin air and then loaned out to the borrowers. So that means, if you deposit Rs. 2,000 into your account and if CRR is 4%, then the banks can create Rs. 1,920 and then lend it out. And all of it will be created with nothing but by typing the numbers into the system (also elucidated in the section on Fractional Reserve Banking).

So, the central bank and government are not backing fiat currencies with anything but IOUs and everybody in the market (except end users, i.e. depositors and borrowers) are swapping IOUs to create new currencies out of thin air. Note, only end borrowers are keeping collateral as their houses but government and commercial banks easily get loans by keeping government securities with the central bank.

This whole cycle has been going on for decades and with the creation of new currency with each passing day, the value of existing money in the market is constantly decreasing. This is leading to inflation.

If we are to find an analogy to this whole system, imagine a big room in which industry stalwarts, RBI governor, Finance Ministry and Government are sitting and exchanging IOUs with each other and creating new currency. That's what is happening here and around the world.

Even though the government can, but it will not make central bank print lots of currency because the system will collapse and people will get to know about this scam, due to a sudden spike in prices in the market. Recall the example of Zimbabwe. Remember, the aim of those at the helm of our institutions, is not to get rich, their aim is to stay rich and powerful. Their aim is to maintain their dominance and power over people.

Thus, new currency is created and prices rise but only at a steady speed, so we continue to work harder and harder and not question the dynamics of power around us.

PART IV

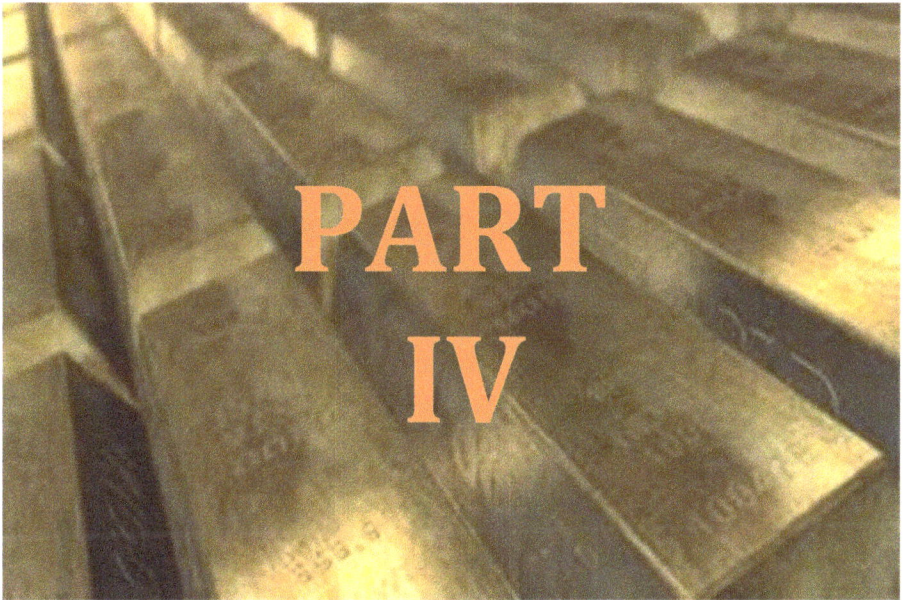

Where Do 'We' Stand – The Case for Gold

It doesn't matter who you are—a business man, a daily wage earner or a government employee—your pockets are going to get lighter as time passes. The present monetary system is designed to devalue currency, i.e. with each passing day the worth of your currency (numbers written on rupee notes) is only going to get smaller for the things that you may want to buy.

It is so because for thousands of years, all governments have debased (devalued) the currency and misused it to pay for public work, social schemes, the war and for anything as per their whims and fancies. It is only going to continue to repeat unless populace senses the fraud and realizes its continuous loss of purchasing power which has been repeating since ages. This eventually leads to bank runs by people to redeem their hard-earned money. Constant rise in prices and this constant loss of people's wealth is an insult to their hard work and creativity. It robs us of our true potential and represents the financial short-sightedness of governments.

Today, we are on the cusp of an economic disaster and financial upheaval, the remnants of which were seen in the 2008 global financial meltdown and many crises before that. Inflation is not only hurting our purchasing power but bringing in the demise of fiat currencies across the world. Loss of people's trust in the institutions would lead to panic (as was evident during the 2016 demonetization as well). This may lead to the collapse of the system in the blink of an eye.

But remember one thing which has been proposed by many analysts before—wealth is never destroyed. After any crisis or economic storm, wealth may change hands and get transferred, but it never gets destroyed. So, it's important that you get to stay on the right side of this wealth transfer and be the beneficiary of it.

How can you be on the right side of wealth transfer? Owning some amounts of gold and silver is a perfect way to hedge against inflation and uncertainties. Demystify this concept of investing in metals. Learn about them, keep yourself informed. They have always been the heavyweight champions in the times of crises. Recall the case of Zimbabwe. When one hundred trillion Zimbabwean dollar currency couldn't save them, it is gold that helped them in carrying on with their lives. Having invested in gold and silver will not only keep you at the top of this wealth transfer but will smash your adversities in their face. Gold is no longer an investment for marriages; it is much more than that. It is the *real* money.

ENDING

"Politicians can't give us anything without depriving us of something else. Government is not god. Every dime they spend must first be taken from someone else. "

~Barry Asmus

During the times of demonetization, bailouts of few wealthy stalwarts and recapitalization of unhealthy assets of banks happened using the taxpayer's money. And who suffered the most? The taxpayer.

A whooping amount of our hard-earned currencies were frozen by the government, thereby bringing our lives to a standstill. If somebody asks them, to what avail? And why our right to property has suddenly vanished into thin air? Why can't I go to the central bank after 31st March 2017 and ask them to exchange my hard-earned currency I might have found somewhere later on? Demonetization did not only shake our lives then, but it continues to be a reminder of annihilation of our rights, and government's and central bank's 'I care a hoot' attitudes towards its people. This realization is the only silver lining that should be taken as a lesson from this 'shock economics' doctrine of demonetization.

If you are an average Indian and someone who works hard, day and night to save some cash in the bank for your children and grandchildren, you are the biggest loser in this deal. Winners are those running these financial institutions and government. They are growing richer and making you poorer, irrespective of how much you work and how well you earn, all that you have accumulate will decrease in value ina span of few years.

When you go to your wholesale dealer and that moment when you notice that the price for a litre of milk has gone up by ten rupees, or when you pay for your electricity bill and see an unexpected rise of Rs. 300, it is an indication of poor performance of our government and central bank.

Everyone I know has had a taste of these experiences, I am sure you or your parents must have had it too. It is a hidden battle which is being waged among the taxpayers and common masses. It is a battle against those at the helm of power, those who are constantly abusing and misusing their privileges with the sole aim of keeping their throne intact. They don't want to get rich, they want to *remain* rich and the only pin which can burst this *jumla* is the power of knowledge. Let's take the reins of our financial freedom back from those abusers.

It wouldn't be wrong to say that today's system is stacked against us, in favour of a few. The only thing which binds it together is our blind trust in these institutions. It gives them an open license for theft! While everyone is obliged to pay their debts, bankers can afford to simply go bankrupt. 2008 anyone? Is it fair?

This is one of the main reasons why Indians have traditionally loved to hold onto gold. Many had little faith in banks and other financial institutions, thus they preferred to store their wealth in something more reliable and tangible.

> *Gold is not just a fetish for the yellow metal, it's much more.*

Until people have gold in their hands, governments will always be reproachful of them. Even with all the power, prestige and trust backing their system, gold has the power to overturn the future of their establishment. Its unique qualities led markets to select them in the first place and it may see golds dawn, as money again.

"Borrowers will default. Markets will collapse. Gold (the ultimate form of state money) will skyrocket. "

~Michael Belkin

Or can we expect to see bits of zeros and ones as the future of currency? May be. Nothing can be said for sure. But one thing is sure; the present Fractional Reserve Banking system is robbing us big-time. Drawing our blood, sweat, and energy and giving us only peanuts in return. We are in an age which may witness the explosion of the biggest bubble of all time –

the bubble of fiat currencies. Going by the spending spree of our governments, that time doesn't seem to be very far.

Hedge yourself against inflation and strengthen your understanding about financial instruments and financial systems by reading relevant books. Don't fear crises. Have a dialogue with them. Fathom them. This new knowledge will take you to a new age of freedom, opportunity and progress.

This book should not be considered as a solicitation of any particular investment product. I want people to make conscious decisions when it comes to investing their intellectual and physical energies. I especially want to alert those who don't have any particular investment plans or means to hedge themselves and their families against inflation.

About the Author

With his revolutionary thoughts and actions, Sachin Mittal has been transforming the way financial investment is looked upon in the new age.

He acquired this revolutionary outlook after having worked for a decade with ICICI Bank as their Corporate Channel Partner and also with different NBFCs.

During his tenure, he developed a stupendous portfolio of approximately Rs. 5000 crores of retail home loans. Many in those days believed that he had become larger than the bank itself.

It was during this journey that he came in contact with the bigwigs of the financial and corporate sector, and this gave him an insight not only into how people acquire wealth but also how they lose it.

He was quick to realize that traditional financial processes were not built for the modern business economy. Therefore, he embraced more strategic, agile and responsive financial investment modules, in-line with the changing times.

A Shining Example of the Open New Age Economy

Mittal is busy bringing about a paradigm shift in financial thoughts as he believes that the knowledge of the last 200 years on the subject is not relevant anymore.

A leading entrepreneur, author, thinker and a poet, Sachin is making his compatriots re-analyze their concepts and thoughts about financial investment. After having studied both engineering and art, he has become a shining example of the new age economy and operates on a global scale.

He soon realized through his experiences that in order to succeed in today's business environment, it was necessary to shift from the old, outdated models of money-making to new techniques keeping in mind the ever-changing and fast-paced new business age.

Sachin operates his business globally, and its success is as much an outcome of his business and financial acumen as it is about his ability to adapt to changing circumstances. He is a true representative of today's open economy, and with his vision and business ideology, he has carved an admirable and enviable position for himself in the world of business.

Making Earning Money Easier for People

Sachin is making earning money easier for people through his fresh and innovative approach on some of the key financial aspects. He is leading by example, and his knowledge on the subject is helping the poor become rich, and the rich become richer.

His tale is about the journey of a man who had the courage to take risks when most people had withdrawn; he braved failure to become a man who continues to inspire many youngsters in the country.

Other books
by Sachin Mittal

THE ABC OF
REAL ESTATE IN INDIA

By Sachin Mittal

Surprisingly, every man's common dream of owning a house directly connects to the real estate sector.

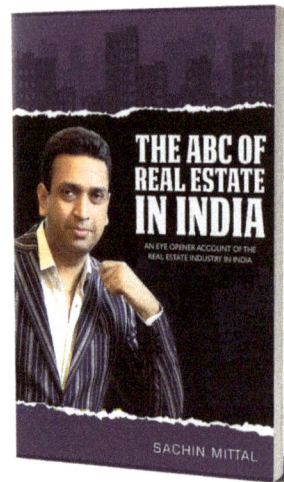

This book has been written to provide the basic information which everyone should possess in order to invest in real estate. It discusses the foundation, dynamics and marketing aspects of the real estate sector and takes the purview of the entire industry.

There is also an equal focus on the customer's point of view and an expert analysis of the customer industry bond. Perhaps, this and many other aspects are inculcated in the book to clarify the importance of the industry in the by lanes of the Indian economy.

Read and find out

THE ABC OF
REAL ESTATE
IN INDIA

AN EYE OPENER ACCOUNT OF THE
REAL ESTATE INDUSTRY IN INDIA

SACHIN MITTAL

HOW THE FUTURE
WILL RESHAPE WORK

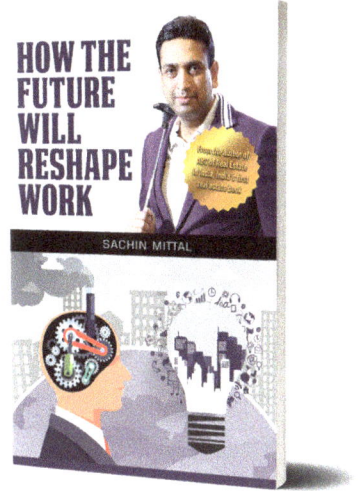

By Sachin Mittal

It is estimated that by 2010 robots will replace about 75 percent of the workforce in the USA

This alone will have a major impact on the shape of work in the future

How prepared are you for it?

We already have cars that drive themselves, machines that read X-Rays. These and many more are examples of the new world of automation

As these continue to improve our lives they will sadly replace the humans who are currently doing these jobs

Only a miniscule 5 percent of the jobs are there which doesn't run the risk of automation

Read and find out more

Price

REWRITING
KISMET

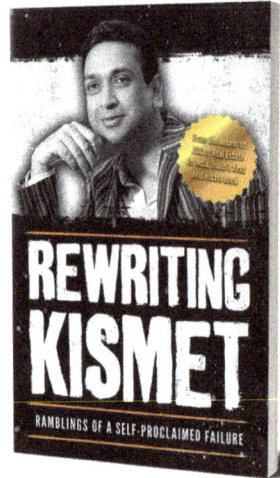

By Sachin Mittal

- ★ Trials are inevitable in life, especially in an entrepreneur's life
- ★ And trials are unique to each one of us
- ★ Yet the blessings of entrepreneurship are special
- ★ It gives entrepreneurs the ability to see solutions before the rest of the world can see
- ★ But if you are a true entrepreneur you will be up to the challenge of putting the pieces back together
- ★ He goes by the belief that you will fail and fail till you can no longer fail
- ★ It is not easy to rescue a failed business

But what can be worse than failing?

- ★ Not trying
- ★ Not trying is worse than failing
- ★ If you never try you will die with the frustration that you have never tried

Read and find out

Upcoming books
by Sachin Mittal

ASSURED RETURNS
IN REAL ESTATE

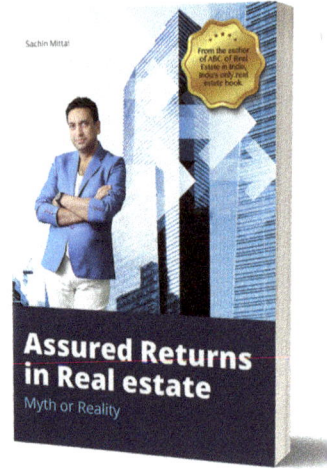

By Sachin Mittal

Are you amongst those who while investing in an under-construction real estate was offered up to 12 percent interest on investment?

Developers call it assured returns, but do you know that if they fail to give you the assured return there is nothing you can do about it.

Can you trust a party who is in a cash crunch situation and promising you fixed monthly cash returns? It has RISKY written all over it.

Why do they offer such schemes?

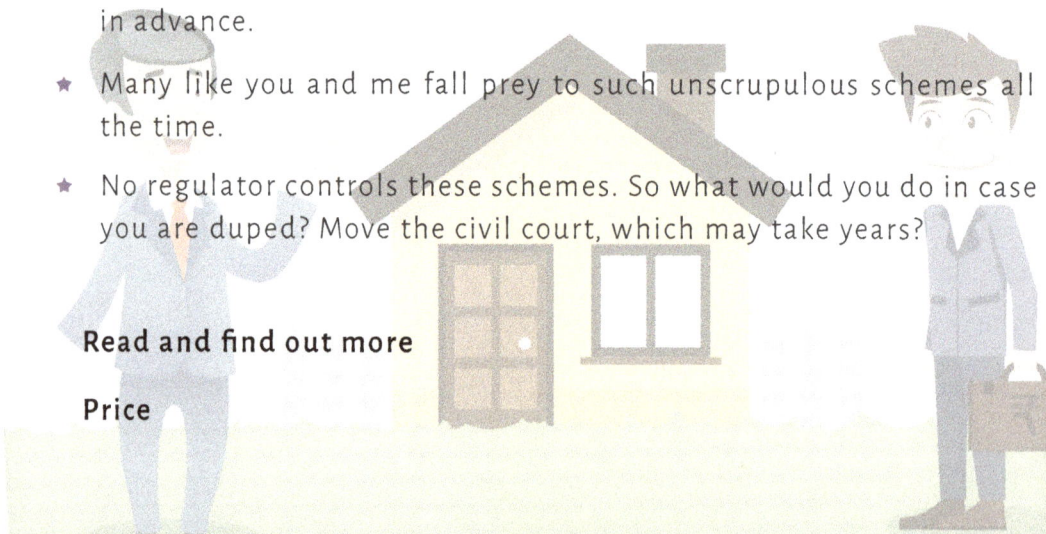

★ They do it for liquid investment and more politically-correct reason given by developers is that these schemes help them to gauge the market sentiments and buyers' readiness to buy their projects right in advance.

★ Many like you and me fall prey to such unscrupulous schemes all the time.

★ No regulator controls these schemes. So what would you do in case you are duped? Move the civil court, which may take years?

Read and find out more

Price

MONEY, LOVE FOOLISHNESS GO TOGETHER

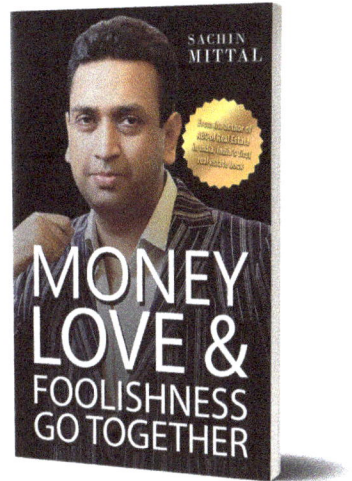

By Sachin Mittal

Worries, debt and love. We are not responsible for their presence. They come uninvited.

Why is it that even the smartest and the most respectable amongst us are caught turning foolish and doing the dumbest of things when in love...or when we have money pouring on us?

It is good to be smart. All smart people are intelligent and make more money. Then how is it that the very same intelligent people behave contrary to their nature when they are in love or when suddenly they acquire wealth beyond their imagination.

Many intelligent people have the reputation of making dumb mistakes. And these dumb mistakes are committed primarily when they are under the influence of money or love.

Agree? No?

Read and find out

Price:

TO BUY OR NOT TO BUY
A HOME

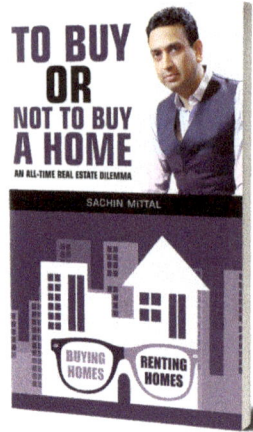

By Sachin Mittal

Have you heard of the saying "fools buy houses and wise men live in them?"
The latest talks doing the rounds is that buying a house is for suckers.

Why so?

* A house is not an investment as it doesn't pay you every month. You will get money when you are old and sell off your house.

* Well...who wants money when he is old?

* Moreover, wouldn't you prefer to be mobile and nimble? Who doesn't want to be?

* These are some of the issues about owned properties. Similarly there are quite a few for rental property.

Read and find out

Price

UNDERSTANDING HOW TO HANDLE HOME LOANS

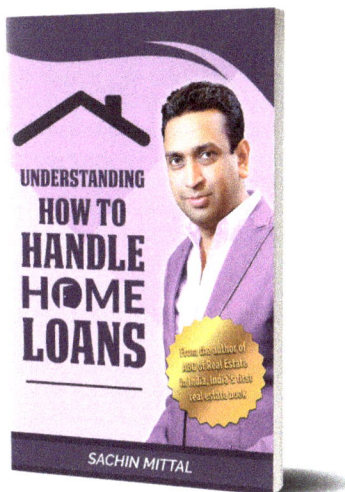

By Sachin Mittal

Did you know that a huge majority of home loan application don't even pass the first stage? Strange but true.

This may be because there is such limited information about how to handle home loans? Maybe because limited knowledge amongst potential borrowers is bliss for bankers/HFCs.

Contrary to what is said in the ads, it is not that easy to get a home loan. There is a myriad of hurdles that need to be resolved.

The volatility in interest rates in India has affected borrowers of all types of loans.

Moreover, there are so many misconceptions and myths about home loans that it is not difficult to fall into their trap.

Buy and read now

Price

www.ingramcontent.com/pod-product-compliance
Lightning Source LLC
Chambersburg PA
CBHW042121190326
41519CB00031B/7574